Tracking is Trending

A Survival Guide to Assessment in Student Affairs

Tracking is Trending

⟵ ⟶

A SURVIVAL GUIDE TO ASSESSMENT IN STUDENT AFFAIRS

KIM IRLAND
· SERIES EDITOR ·

TOM KRIEGLSTEIN, SABINA DE MATTEO,
JUHI BHATT & ALEX FIELDS
· BOOK EDITORS ·

ILLUSTRATED BY SUE CAULFIELD

Tracking is Trending

A Survival Guide to Assessment in Student Affairs

Collaboratively Created By

Kim Irland – Series Editor

Sue Caulfield – Illustrator

Juhi Bhatt – Book Editor

Alex Fields – Book Editor

Sabina De Matteo – Book Editor

Tom Krieglstein – Book Editor

Other Student Affairs Collective Books

Trust the Journey - When and How to Move for Your Student Affairs Career

Beyond Meetings – Lessons and Success in Advising Student Organizations

Men in Student Affairs - Stories from 13 Student Affairs Professionals

From the Beginning: Perspectives from New and Emerging SA Pros

Hello My Name Is Committed: Stories About Dealing with Mental Illness in Student Affairs

All titles can be viewed and ordered at
www.StudentAffairsCollective.org/Bookstore

Student Affairs Collective
www.StudentAffairsCollective.org
info@studentaffairscollective.org
Phone: (877) 479-4385
Fax: (206) 337-0259

>> Contact for bulk order discounts <<

About The Student Affairs Collective

As with all great ideas, the Student Affairs Collective (www.StudentAffairsCollective.org) began as a series of doodles on the back of a napkin by Tom Krieglstein and Kevin Prentiss in 2005. The vision was, and still is, to create the ultimate online community of student affairs professionals in which everyone is both a teacher and student at the same time to help each other play, learn and grow together to collectively reach higher levels of success.

In the beginning, Tom and Kevin wrote all the content. They then bribed their student affairs friends with cookies and digital unicorns to help them write more content, and slowly, over time, an engaged community developed. The SA Collective started to become the go-to place online for student affairs professionals to receive and share knowledge from their peers. The growth remained steady, and then Twitter came along...

In 2009, over lunch with Debra Sanborn at an Iowa coffee shop, Tom pitched the idea of a weekly chat via Twitter for student affairs professionals. Debra nodded excitedly at the idea (as she does with all new ideas), and a couple weeks later, on Oct 8th, 2009, the first #SAChat happened with 15 people and 50 tweets.

Since then, the SAC, which is what the cool kids call it, has grown to be a community of thousands of student affairs professionals, stretching international borders and all functional areas of the field. We now have a podcast, a book club, a jobs board, a member directory with learning communities, a weekly newsletter, Tweetups, and the #SAChat Awards. Through it all, the SAC continues to focus on creating the best online, low cost, peer-to-peer learning network for student affairs professionals.

Now it's your turn to jump in and be a part of the family and help us create the next ten years of awesomeness. As a bonus, you'll laugh, smile, create friendships, and grow a positive national reputation for yourself and your work. Then, when you go on to change the world, we'll get to say you first shared your potential with us by helping fellow student affairs professionals be even more amazing!

Tom Krieglstein
Founder, Student Affairs Collective
@TomKrieglstein

How To Use This Book

While this entire book is focused around one main theme, each individual author takes on a unique perspective around the main theme. Some chapters might be totally relevant to your current situation and others not so much. Reading this book from beginning to end is probably not going to be as valuable as looking at the table of contents and skipping ahead to the chapters that are most relevant to your current situation.

Share The Love Online

We love seeing when fellow student affairs professionals take their professional development into their own hands. If you take a photo of you with this book and share it online via one of the channels listed below, we'll send you digital unicorns in return!

On Twitter post your photo using one of these two methods:
Use the #SAChat hashtag
Tag the @The_SA_Blog account

On Facebook post your photo to one of these two groups:
Student Affairs Professionals >
https://www.facebook.com/groups/2204795643/
Student Affairs Collective >
https://www.facebook.com/SACollective

Introducing

Real-Time Assessment Analytics

Identify trends & understand behaviors with
real-time assessment analytics mixed with
student attributes and demographics.

Learn More at CheckImHere.com

The Assessment Series, and this book, were supported by Check I'm Here.

To the collaborators

Writers, I strongly agree your contributions to this book are outstanding. No seriously, jokes aside, I believe peer facilitated learning, whatever the topic, is so immensely valuable in Student Affairs. That's why we all love "borrowing/stealing" each other's best practices! Please keep writing and sharing your brilliance. You all have so much knowledge and individualism to bring to the table. Pride yourself on your insights!

Student Affairs Collective staff, especially Tom, Sabina, and Juhi, I am incredibly humbled to work with you on creating space for conversations between colleagues. Compiling the assessment conversation in this book was true collaboration, and I'm so grateful to be a part of the work you do.

Shaun, thank you for your patience and support when I get consumed writing or editing posts for SAC at home. I'm so grateful to have a spouse who is proud of my professional identity as well as my home one.

Kim Irland
@kimantics

table of contents
- - - - - - - - - - - - - - - - -

Introduction

Tracking is trending folks. It's the data collection age and assessment is everyone's favorite, right? Okay, so let's agree that while assessment probably isn't your favorite, its bad reputation is a bit unfair, too, like the state of New Jersey's. Wink.

This book will treat you to a variety of knowledgeable and relatable perspectives on assessment as a state of mind, a culture, a story, and yes, as an imperative. No matter what realm of Student Affairs you practice in, assessment absolutely matters. It matters because we all need to look for ways to continuously improve our services, practices, and programs. It matters because assessment informs our institutional and functional area planning. It matters because student learning outside the classroom needs to be measured in order to demonstrate that we are reaching our intended learning outcomes. And perhaps most anxiety producing of late, while enrollment declines at higher education institutions of all sizes across the country, it matters because it helps us justify funding for personnel and resources, reinforcing our value as student affairs educators.

I'm sure many of you would agree that assessment is not solely the responsibility of offices of institutional research or personnel whose titles include "assessment." We all share this role and should seek opportunities for cross-training in this area when possible. We all add value to the assessment process because of our diversified perspectives.

As you read through these chapters, we hope you will gain inspiring insights and take time to reflect on how you make meaning of your data collection and assessment practices. And be sure to follow the ongoing conversation and share your thoughts on Twitter with #SAassess.

Now, on a scale of one to five, how ready are you to read?

Overcoming the "I Don't Have Time" Barrier - Megan Foreki, Jessica Litvak, and Lucas Schalewski

Often times, student affairs professionals have a desire to conduct assessment but when questioned on why assessment is not being completed, the response "I don't have time," is a leading answer.

As professionals who have been there ourselves, the following tips supported us through the assessment process. It is our hope that these takeaways will provide new strategies to those who find themselves struggling, or know of colleagues who struggle, with completing assessment due to not having time.

Assessment as a Catch-22

Assessment is paradoxical in the sense that to help identify where you can find more time in order to do assessment, one must do assessment.

Good assessment benefits you in the long term as it informs your practice. It allows us to provide intentional and meaningful programs and services to students. If you have ever wondered whether or not a program or service is actually effective and worth the time you put into it, quality assessment will give you the answers you seek. These insights will direct your yearly strategic plans, as you can clearly identify strengths and weaknesses to funnel your time in ways that meet the intended student outcomes. **It's all about working smarter with assessment, not harder, to make the most of your time as a resource.**

"It's all about working smarter with assessment, not harder, to make the most of your time as a resource."

Find Your Assessment Zone

For some practitioners, our offices can be inundated with students, colleagues, and emails that keep piling on, which makes it hard to focus on designing assessment. Chat with your supervisor, schedule an hour or two in a morning or afternoon, and set up your mobile office at your favorite coffee spot or location around campus! **Dedicate that time to clearing your mind of your other professional responsibilities, and find your assessment zone.** Sometimes you need to find a new space to refocus your mind and get creative!

Know Where to Start and Do So Modestly

Thinking about assessment may feel overwhelming at first. That leads many to the inaccurate conclusion of not having enough time. In these cases, the "I don't have time" response may really mean, "I don't know where to start." Take a few deep breaths before starting an assessment project and find ways to relax – You can do this! **Identifying the couple of steps to begin assessment helps to create a focused plan that will lead to successful assessment.**

To begin, identify one program or service that you want to assess – do not feel like you need to create an assessment for your whole office/department right from the start. Once you have identified a program or service, answer the question: "What do you want to know about that program or service?" Now that you know where to start, you are better able to move forward and not feel so overwhelmed, which may lead to the "I don't have time" barrier. These first couple of steps is where you should start, and will support you in creating an assessment plan!

Create a Plan

Not everyone is a planner, but when it comes to assessment it certainly helps. **A well-developed assessment plan is able to help ensure you complete assessment by effectively closing the loop.** Assessment may seem at first like a lot of time, but when you see it written down as an assessment plan, you will recognize that it is very much doable. An assessment plan is based on the cycle of assessment, which helps you manage your time in a well-crafted manner.

After you have developed an assessment plan for one program or service, it becomes much easier to design a plan for others. If you get really stuck, that is okay! Identify other assessment experts around campus who may be able to steer you in the right direction.

Make Friends with an Assessment Guru

Save time by identifying and getting to know the assessment gurus on your campus. **If you are unsure of how to write a learning outcome or thinking about methods of data collection, assessment experts and champions are there to help you.**

If you do not have an assessment office in student affairs, there is likely a colleague who has a lot of experience in this area. If you already know whom this assessment champion is, invite them out to lunch or coffee as a way to intentionally build that professional relationship and support. Trust us, assessment gurus love to talk about assessment and will likely welcome the invitation!

Talk to Your Supervisor

Conveying the relationship between assessment and your unit/department's goals and responsibilities to your supervisor is a helpful strategy to find time for assessment. Ask your supervisor to hold you accountable with assessment, and clearly communicate its importance to your work. After chatting with your supervisor, they should be more willing (and excited!) to support you in taking time for assessment, and even involving you in other assessment professional opportunities!

Quick Tips and Tricks to Find More Time for Assessment

- Use your breaks in your work cycle wisely! If you find more availability during summer, use that time to create an assessment plan.
- It takes two to tango! Partner up with a colleague on an assessment project.
- Use student workers to save time on data collection, analysis, and communication of results. Graduate assistants and interns are helpful as well!
- Schedule some time on your calendar.

- Find the joy in assessment and make it fun for you.
- Stop assessing outcomes that you are not finding meaningful or useful in your work. Use that time for more purposeful assessment.

Lucas is at the University of Arizona. He is passionate about advancing purposeful outcome-based assessment for the demonstration and improvement of student learning and development.

Megan serves the University of Arizona. In her role, she oversees volunteer programs, including Alternative Breaks, as well as assessment efforts for the Associated.

Jessica is at University of Arizona. Jessica's role works to effectively build partnerships between student affairs and academic affairs at UA with the common goal of fostering students' connection to the institution at large.

WHAT DO WE DO WITH THIS DATA?
assessment for meaningful change

What Do We Do With This Data? Assessment for
Meaningful Change - Lisa Endersby

Write the survey. Get feedback. Write it again
(and again and again). Distribute the survey. Remind
people to fill in the survey (again and again and again).
Get the results. Compile the results. Report the results.
Rinse. Repeat.
We've travelled this path before.

While an important and increasingly popular method of
evaluation, **the assessment cycle can quickly become a
closed feedback loop, running perpetually on Likert
scales and annual reports.** We have become very good
at collecting and reporting data (or, at the very least,
acknowledging how vital it is to do it), **but don't often
or always use what we learn to recommend and enact
positive change for our departments, programs, and
students.**

> "The assessment cycle can quickly become a closed feedback loop, running perpetually on Likert scales and annual reports."

One lingering resistance to attempting to make change based on assessment results is time, or lack thereof. There just isn't time or space to add attempting to overhaul an entire program based on the same (small) group of students sharing the same (biased) feedback.

What worries me most about these and similar concerns is the pervasive all-or-nothing approach to assessment. **One survey doesn't make or break a program, just as one bad day doesn't make for a bad life.** Meaningful and positive transformation from assessment results is easier when we begin to challenge some of our favorite assumptions about change.

Change is good... sometimes

I may be contradicting myself, but, sometimes, assessment isn't about change. **Sometimes assessment is about validating that we're on the right track.** Other times it's a chance to collect information about our students that may inform what we do next. Sometimes our desire to appear innovative, responsive, and productive means change happens for change's sake. It looks good to change – to change big and change often. However, constant change is more confusing than constructive. Don't change because you're supposed to; change because you must or because it's time.

That being said...

Change takes time, needs time, and doesn't happen all the time

True, meaningful change doesn't happen overnight. Or over several nights. There are even times when you begin to change but move on before the change is implemented. Productive change needs time to be discussed and space to grow. We often race to make change, either to get it over with or to make it happen before anyone else notices what's happening. Neither is good for your workload (or sanity), and both are extremely detrimental to the relationships you have developed. Time is not the enemy – it is not only your students that will benefit, but also many of the students who will come after.

Change isn't about you

If I could offer one, and only one, piece of advice to anyone afraid of assessment, it would be this. Assessment isn't personal. Survey results aren't about you. A dismal program evaluation is a reflection of so many other things, least of which are your competency or compassion. **We so often resist change of any sort because it means admitting defeat, or that scary F-word: failure.** I am far more impressed by someone willing to acknowledge challenges and move forward, rather than someone expending finite energy on appearing 'perfect'. Yes, we have an obligation to stakeholders. Yes, there is pressure to perform. But we cannot perform if we waste energy on chasing the ideal of perfection. Sadly, perfection does not and will never exist; not for our programs and not for us. **Change is for the greater good, not to look good.**

Data is the fuel that drives our assessment cycle, but critical reflection and authentic analysis take the wheel. We can choose to drive the same circular path, going through the motions and staying comfortable, or we can — with intention, patience, and an eye to the future — blaze our own trails.

A voracious reader from a young age, I (attempt to) balance living in my own head with externally processing anything and everything with anyone and everyone. Taking on the title of 'Advocate for Awesome', my work in higher education spans defining and chasing student success in leadership development, career services, community engagement and, my most recent love, assessment. Follow her on twitter @lmendersby

4 STAGES OF ASSESSMENT COMPETENCE

Four Stages of Assessment Competence - Gavin Henning

The statement below has been my mantra for the past five years. **Too often, assessment is seen as an afterthought** rather than an integral part of the program or service planning and implementation process.

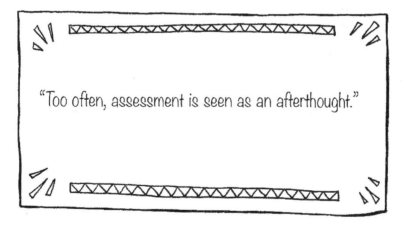

"Too often, assessment is seen as an afterthought."

Interestingly, this statement didn't occur to me when I was in the midst of an assessment project, teaching class, facilitating a workshop, or consulting with a division of student affairs. It occurred to me in a grocery store. Yes, in the deli aisle waiting on maple and brown sugar ham, to be exact.

I don't want to talk about the statement itself, but rather what it represents. Recently, I echoed this refrain during a webinar sponsored by ACPA's Commission for Assessment and Evaluation. The topic was **"Assessing Cultures of Assessment."** At the outset, I suggested that this statement, "Assessment isn't an activity. It's a state of mind," was a definitive sign that a culture of assessment existed in an organization. **When assessment is a state of mind, it is infused into every aspect of individual or organizational practice including planning, implementation, and – of course – evaluation.** At this stage, assessment becomes an unconscious, embedded element of everyday work.

So, how does one arrive at this destination where assessment is a state of mind?
I think the four stages of competence, originally described as the four stages of learning, and outlined by

Linda Adams (2011), can be a helpful guide. These stages are:

- Unconscious incompetence
- Conscious incompetence
- Conscious competence
- Unconscious competence

In the **unconscious incompetence** stage, people are not yet engaged in assessment and don't know why it's important. They are unable to articulate its value or purpose. This stage described most of our Student Affairs field 10-15 years ago. **The prevailing attitude was that assessment was simply a fad and we just needed to "wait it out."**

Once awakened to both the necessity and benefit of engaging in assessment, people realized they need to do it, but some are still not sure how to do it. This is **conscious incompetence.** The first step is to identify the actual skills and knowledge needed to perform assessment. The 2nd Edition of the ACPA/NASPA Professional Competencies (released in August 2015) provides a framework for skill and knowledge development regarding assessment, evaluation, and research.

A great way to develop assessment skills is to seek out books, workshops, and other resources to improve skill and knowledge. Fortunately, more and more resources are available. There are four new student affairs assessment books coming out this academic year (2015-2016). How exciting! One centers on leading assessment for student success and the other focuses on coordinating divisional assessment. Two more covering more general assessment practice will come out in early March 2016. Workshops and conferences are another way to build assessment competence.

Each summer, ACPA holds its **Student Affairs Assessment Institute** and NASPA sponsors its **Assessment and Persistence Conference**. Both associations have special interest groups regarding assessment for networking and professional development. (ACPA's Commission for Assessment and Evaluation and NASPA's Assessment, Evaluation, and Research Knowledge Community). In addition, many master's level preparation programs have assessment courses to help students move from this stage of competence to the next.

As people gain skill and knowledge, they become **conscious competent**. They value the assessment process and are continually attentive when performing it. Assessment takes effort and concentration at this stage but continues to become more comfortable and more frequent.

At the apex of this competence hierarchy is **unconscious competence**. At this stage, assessment has been performed so often that it becomes habit or second nature and is integrated into daily practice and processes. It is important to note that learning should still take place. Even in assessment, lifelong learning is important as new scholarship is constantly being created.

As I mentioned at the beginning, the statement "Assessment isn't an activity. It's a state of mind" came to me in a grocery store. In the deli aisle, I recognized that I was shopping in a way that mirrored the assessment process. My goal was to be both effective and efficient and those goals shaped my actions from planning to execution. Assessment had become so unconscious that it was integrated into other parts of my life. While, you may not be as much of a geek as me and want assessment to infiltrate your personal life, I do hope you develop your assessment skill and knowledge to the point that you are **unconsciously competent**.

At what stage are you? What can you do to get to the next level? Adams, L. (2011). Learning a new skill is easier said than done. [Blog]. Retrieved from http://goo.gl/iM2iv

Gavin is a college student educator with a reputation as an organizer, collaborator, and catalyst for educational change. Gavin holds a Doctor of Philosophy degree in Education Leadership and Policy Studies and a Master of Arts degree in Sociology both from the University of New Hampshire as well as a Master of Arts degree in College and University Administration and a Bachelor of Science degree in Psychology and Sociology from Michigan State University.

Assessment: Challenge(s) Accepted - Jeff Kegolis and
Maria Marinucci

The act of conducting assessment as part of one's weekly responsibilities may often feel like an afterthought for student affairs professionals. Certain staff may even use some of their favorite Freudian defense mechanisms like denial, repression, or avoidance, just to name a few, as they shift to other "priorities." But have no fear! We will aim to coach you on **balancing assessment with putting out the fires that keep our week far from predictable,** while helping you to **reframe your current approach to prioritization** that may be focused too closely on an upcoming major event/program/process appearing on next month's horizon.

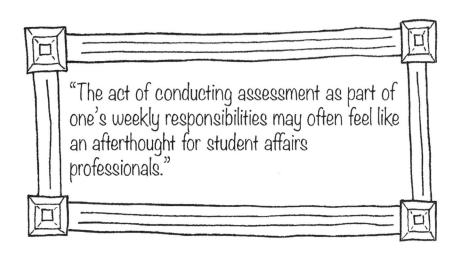

"The act of conducting assessment as part of one's weekly responsibilities may often feel like an afterthought for student affairs professionals."

As one begins to consider how to conduct effective assessment, **it's important to understand how your team's/functional area's approach complements the overall practice at your institution.** Additionally, it's critical to appreciate how capturing learning in your area further supports a commitment to the students we serve and the experience they should receive as part of their decision to enroll. Overall, **assessment is a tool to ensure learning is taking place,** and that we have evidence of how our daily operations enhance the experiences of our students. To support you in your efforts, and after reflecting on the work of colleagues within our divisional assessment team, we have identified 4 common challenges, with proposed solutions to consider as you aim to create best practices:

Challenge #1: "I am the only person in my department that knows how to do assessment, and I just cannot do it all."

Solution: Teach/Train Staff on What is Effective Assessment

It seems intuitive, but the best way to do the work is to **share the work.** If possible and you don't have one already, **convene a divisional assessment team.** Each time you meet, have a different department share how they are assessing their work, and allow others to comment or offer suggestions. Through this process, one of our functional areas that had very limited understanding of assessment learned through their attendance and participation on this committee.

As meetings progress in the academic year, ask questions of one another to gain a broader mix of perspectives and **establish synergy**. If you cannot do an entire divisional meeting, schedule time with colleagues from other departments and ask them what they are doing. Then, take what you learn back to your own department and delegate assessment tasks– Who will write the plan? Who will create the assessment tool? Who will analyzes the results? Then, all together, **"close the loop"** and plan how you will use the results to improve practice.

Challenge #2: "My colleagues say they don't have time to do assessment work."

Solution: Model that Assessment is a Priority

A mentor once told me **how you spend your time and what you commit your budget to speak to what you prioritize.** You may have also seen the quote, "what you allow, is what will continue." If you catch yourself saying "there isn't enough time for assessment," then it's because it hasn't been embraced or modeled as a priority. **Starting today, schedule weekly blocks of time where you spend time on assessment.** The key is creating momentum for your efforts. As the law of momentum states, an object in motion will stay in motion until it meets a resisting force. Once assessment becomes a habit it will become easier to incorporate. Succeed with assessment by controlling how you spend your time. Keep pushing forward.

Challenge #3: "Those in my department see assessment as just another requirement, rather than something actually connected to our practice." or "We know our students are (not) satisfied...but that's about it."

Solution: Map Learning Outcomes to Department Goals and Get Back to Basics (i.e., learning)

In some ways, this challenge connects to the previous issue (i.e., how assessment is viewed). One can begin to appreciate that if assessment is prioritized, then it will be done effectively. However, it is critical for staff to **view assessment as having a ripple effect on what we do instead of perceiving it as an annoying requirement.**

One way to embrace assessment is by **having a monthly meeting within one's functional area to share evidence of learning or conclusions that have been reached as a result of analyzing data.** Other possibilities may include: focus groups that support your ongoing efforts (e.g., marketing of programs) and surveys that capture direct learning (e.g., direct learning could be used comparatively from year to year to determine the effectiveness of skills taught or curriculum utilized). **The key is to continue to identify connections based on what you've done, to what you've learned, to what you'll keep or change** (i.e., embracing the ripple effect). Through this approach, staff will begin to understand that assessment efforts pay off, and deduce that assessment actually matters!

Challenge #4: "Others outside our department don't care about our results, so it seems pointless."

Solution: Connect to Your Strategic Plan

Most leadership books encourage the idea of catching staff in the act of doing something good. However, most of us will agree that celebrations will not occur around results from a survey or the evidence we've compiled to show the effectiveness of our work. Despite others not being excited about it, **it's important**

to focus on how as a functional area we can improve our efforts and accomplish our goals.

If a team begins to focus on their strategic plan, then they can begin to work toward the same goals. Additionally, collaboration will likely be enhanced within one's team or within the division to reach these goals. Recently at our university, when a functional area was struggling with why they should even do assessment, a new director tied the process to larger institutional priorities. This not only created enthusiasm around the staff's work, making the team feel part of something bigger, it helped everyone feel re-energized about other considerations they had been moving toward. Overall, this simple connection catapulted their efforts forward in a manner that, using the previous approach, would have left them lost or taken months to achieve.

> "Planning is bringing the future into the present so that you can do something about it now." – Alan Lakein

In closing, there will always be challenges with conducting effective assessment. Reframing your priority list, using synergy with assessment, and working towards a vision with clear goals where your assessment serves as evidence for change, are critical approaches to use. As we adopt our practices based on efforts to transform students through their experiences, it is important for us to **take pride in what we do and elevate our practices.** Keeping in mind that as Tony Robbins said, "change is inevitable, progress is optional."

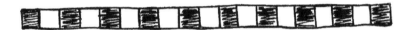

 Dr. Jeff Kegolis serves as the Director of Student Conduct & Assessment at the University of Scranton. Jeff received his Ph.D. in higher education administration from Bowling Green State University. Maria R. Marinucci serves as the Assistant Director for Residence Education in Residence Life at The University of Scranton. She received her bachelor's degree in psychology from Colgate University and her master's degree in student affairs in higher education from Colorado State University.

Setting the Groundwork - Four Steps for the SSAO -

Kayley Robsham

Believe it or not, assessment has been around longer than you may think. In fact, it's been around since student affairs played a role in formal and informal student learning. In the past decade, it has evolved to fit the needs of the ever-changing traits of today's college student and has shaped learning outcomes to engage students in profound ways.

Accomplishing assessment tasks across a division or department is no easy feat. **In order to accurately measure student learning, assessment must be integrated into work of all student affairs staff.** How do we create and sustain a culture of assessment at institutions of higher education? Who is responsible for spearheading assessment initiatives? Where does it start?

"In order to accurately measure student learning, assessment must be integrated into work of all student affairs staff."

Here are four considerations when starting to on-board assessment practices with professionals on your team:

1. Start at the top.

It's difficult to create expectations around assessment when senior student affairs officers (SSAOs) do not value them. According to Seagraves and Dean (2010), **creating a culture of assessment from senior leadership is most important to the longevity and success of any**

assessment initiative. Here are some of the best ways to implement them from a senior role:

- Approach assessment with a positive attitude
- Provide adequate training and resources for your team
- Incorporate expectations of assessment into job descriptions and performance evaluations
- Create an assessment committee or block time for check-ins during regularly scheduled meetings
- Use data collected from your team, determine priorities, and determine how to improve practices on both a micro and macro scale

2. Break it down.

Assessment doesn't have to be a dirty word. Resources put towards assessment do not need to be terribly extensive either, but they do require staff time and resources. As a manager or supervisor at any level, it's important to explain the exact materials you and your team will be using to conduct assessment practices throughout the year. **Taking time at the beginning of the year to clearly layout the foundation of assessment practices will help in the long term when compiling reports or evaluating programs.**

3. Train, train, train.

Talk the talk, walk the walk. If you're highlighting how important assessment is to your department and you don't train your staff, you may run into a few hiccups down the road. **Providing the tools and training for student affairs practitioners is vital for their success at conducting assessment in an effective way.** Additionally, if your department or division is new to assessment, it will further help with on-boarding professionals who may be resistant to change.

4. Share the responsibility.

When one person is solely responsible for assessment, it won't become a sustainable process. For example, if that person happens to leave the institution, it will be hard to provide continuous assessment and pass on knowledge accrued from that person to the next. **Creating a system of how data will be collected and knowledge will be shared will make practices transparent and accessible for the entire team.**

SSAOs have the important role of sustaining assessment processes at their institution due to their informed perspective of strategic goals of both their direct reports and the university at large. Senior leaders of divisions or departments have the ability to articulate assessment activities and share results with other departments or divisions to make a large impact at all levels. Although a shared obligation among all staff, senior leadership sets the tone of making assessment a priority at the institution.

What are some ways you've on-boarded assessment practices to your division or department? How have you shared responsibilities among your team?

 Kayley Robsham is a twenty-something woman working at Check I'm Here, a HigherEd technology software company, as the Community Engagement Manager. She enjoys exploring new coffee shops in St. Pete, practicing yoga and meditation, and learning about women in the workplace. F ollow her @kayleyrobsham.

Own It! Recognizing YOUR Responsibility - Joseph Levy

Please indulge me with a quick reflection on behalf of your office/area with the following:

How can you be a better steward of resources?

Are you improving quality of services/programs where necessary?

Are you providing the support needed for students to be retained and successful?

What student trends or issues are emerging to which you need to adjust?

How can you articulate what you do to outside parties?

What are students learning?

Regardless of the office or area you belong at your institution, I am going to assume you are concerned with, would like to know the answer to, or are responsible for answering at least three of those questions. This assumption comes from my experience working with various offices from 60+ institutions. **If these questions apply to you or your work, then you have assessment work to do.** Don't like that conclusion? Take it up with Upcraft and Schuh (2001), as they provide ample documentation and description of how those questions (and more) can be answered with a comprehensive assessment plan. Moreover, if you work hard assembling arguments that those questions don't apply to you; perhaps you are in the wrong line of work.

> "If these questions apply to you or your work, then you have assessment work to do."

While it may not be articulated in your job description or you may not shoulder the entire assessment burden for your area, we'll continue operating on the assumption that assessment applies to you. With that in mind, the most important step you can take at this point is to **own the reality and recognize the responsibility.** Academic affairs/curricular assessment work should be owned and led by faculty. Consequently, student affairs/co-curricular assessment work should be owned and led by staff per area. The subject matter experts for a given office, service, or program are the best people to evaluate and act on data for their area. Assessment staff bring experience working with areas across the university, but their role is to support, guide, and enable resources and structure for quality assessment work to occur, not to do all the work or make all the decisions.

Allow me to state it another way. **Assessment is not "Joe's project" or "Joe's priority" – it should be your project and your priority.** We already agreed assessment applies to you and your work, so you can't use that excuse. Moreover, do you really want someone else interpreting what data says about your programs and making decisions about your office while you just provide peripheral input? I'd hope not! I'd hope you care enough about your area and feel empowered enough to want to be in the decision-maker seat with colleagues and assessment people as your co-pilots.

Once you own assessment, life can become a lot easier for you. Here are a variety of pieces that can fall in place:

- **Assessment planning becomes more intentional.** Knowing this needs to be balanced among your other responsibilities, you will be more intentional planning timelines and resources for assessment since it must fit with other initiatives. When it's not your project, it is easy to allow it to fall to the wayside or allow it to get lost in the shuffle among your other efforts.

- **It'll be easier to onboard colleagues and staff.** When you have the responsibility for a project, you care about it. You'll make a much better pitch to others in that case, as opposed to trying to recruit people for a project you don't even feel involved in.

- **You will take advantage of assessment resources/colleagues.** Just because you recognize the responsibility does not mean you magically inherit assessment knowledge or skills. However, being accountable to conduct assessment projects, you will be more likely to seek out and engage with assessment resources and colleagues in order to complete your work.

- **You can be(come) a data-driven decision maker.** A critical part to the assessment process is using data for continuous quality improvement. Actively participating and owning the process means you will have ample evidence and data to consider when sharing information about your area or making decisions on programs and services.

Assessment may not carry positive connotations for you currently, and that's all right. Look to do the work. Once you do, I would hope the ability of seeing data that answers questions you have or provides evidence of the great work you are doing gives you a sense of satisfaction (and meets reporting needs). More than that, I would hope it empowers you to continue doing this work. I wouldn't be surprised if you develop a genuine curiosity and excitement to review results and draw conclusions. If nothing else, you will make assessment colleagues happy and proud to work with you, forming even stronger bonds doing quality, collaborative assessment work.

Joe Levy is the Sr. Assessment Manager for Co-Curricular Assessment at the University of Phoenix. Joe has worked locally on campuses, as well as served as a consultant for various institutions to lead, foster, and develop strong and successful cultures of assessment. Joe is passionate about data-driven decision making, accountability, and promoting a student-centered approach inside and outside of the classroom. Connect with Joe on Twitter @joebookslevy

IT STARTS WITH
C U R I O S I T Y

It Starts With Curiosity - Lesley D'Souza

Originally posted at www.RyersonStudentAffairs.com on September 30, 2015 as part of the on-going series, Assessment & You.

What is assessment?

Assessment. You've been hearing that word a lot lately in student affairs (unless you're plugging your fingers in your ears and humming your favourite song to avoid assessment-related anxiety). Let's talk about that.

Assessment starts with curiosity, wondering if the work you do all day is actually making a difference. Is it contributing to your goals? What about the goals of your unit or department? How about the institution? We can figure out all of these things simply by asking questions, being observant, writing it down, and trying to use that information to be better at what we do - which is all assessment really is.

To begin with, there are a few different types of assessment:

> **Needs** - Who are we serving? What do they need/like?
>
> **Scope** - What is the reach of our program/service?
>
> **Satisfaction** - Do students like what we have to offer?
>
> **Outcomes** - What do we want to accomplish? Did we do it?
>
> **Benchmarking** - How do we compare to other similar programs/services?
>
> **Standards** - What standards have been set by professional associations? Do we meet them?

You have probably asked at least one of those questions in your day-to-day work. If you take the time to record the answer, you're already doing assessment. Congratulations!

The field of student affairs struggled in the past to come up with consistency and variety in the kinds of data we produce that define the impact of our practices. Our work at Ryerson supports the academic mission of the university, but it has been, at times, challenging to articulate exactly how. When we had fewer students and programs to support them, it was easier to get by with just attendance numbers and anecdotal data. Now, in an increasingly resource-scarce environment, and serving the largest and most demanding student population yet, we must develop consistent and effective cycles of assessment to be sure we're investing our resources right. We can't rely on our passion alone to convince decision-makers because we're all passionate. We need to make their jobs easier by showing them clear measurements to support our case. And really, what's a court case without evidence?

What are we afraid of?

When you hear the word assessment, it can feel like just another thing that you have to find time for in your jam-packed workday. In reality, good assessment shouldn't add much to what you're already doing. It boils down to improving our planning processes and documenting better. If we can work smartly, we won't need to work harder than we already are.

Talking about data can easily induce anxiety for many of us. Assessment and accountability are often spoken in the same breath, and that can definitely make it seem scary. While accountability and justification are real, we shouldn't lose sight of the real goal of assessment—to make ourselves the best we can be. Instinctively, we know what we do does make a difference, but where does that instinct really come from? The good news is that it's probably coming from assessment that you're already doing and just not actually documenting. If you host an event and count the number of people in the room, look around to observe body language, and listen in on conversations; you're already conducting both quantitative and qualitative assessment. From there it's a very short step to conducting assessment in a more mindful way so you can gather more and better data.

We've come a long way in terms of how we plan and assess our work, but there are still many gains to be made. In student affairs we deal in transformational experiences, which, by nature, are difficult to quantify. However, the wonder of assessment is that it doesn't only consist of numbers, stats, and surveys. There are many techniques designed to collect information from conversations, stories, and correlative data that will humanize quantitative data so that it is truly powerful.

But really, why do I need to care?

The benefits of assessment are many and significant. By aligning ourselves more closely to Ryerson's strategic goals, we can position ourselves to be part of conversations that will shape the student experience, and the future of our own work. I participated in a resource and budgeting webinar a couple of years ago, and the most impactful statement I took away was that you don't need to look at a mission statement to best understand an institution's priorities; just look a the budget. We put funding towards things we care about, and we use data to tell us what those things are.

On an individual level, doing good assessment helps us become experts in our work. Just take a look at our own Staff Competencies and you can see where our priorities should be. Assessment isn't going anywhere; becoming proficient at incorporating it into the workday will make us stronger professionals and leaders in student affairs. Planning assessments ahead of programming also helps us by ensuring that we have some control over our work. Data is what will help us build a case to explain what we do and how we do it. I like to think of assessment as the friend who has my back.

Above all, it's a journey and not a destination. We know that learning and development are complex and ever changing, which means our assessments have to be ongoing and comprehensive to give us a complete picture. But don't worry, we're in this together— whether you're an experienced assessor or a newbie— and collectively we can learn and grow.

Lesley is the Student Life Programs Coordinator at Ryerson. She is a passionate, data-driven Student Affairs Professional with an MA in College Student Personnel who loves stories and empowering self-authorship in students. She's the mother of two wonderful boys and an avid gardener, tea drinker, musician and random fact junkie. Ask her anything! She hopes to write a book someday, do her PhD and inspire others. Tweeting from @lesleydsz.

FUNCTIONAL AREA REVIEW

Go FAR - The Functional Area Review - Kimberly Irland

The **Functional Area Review** (FAR) is an assessment practice unique to Jamestown Community College, but it shouldn't be. Its purpose, simply put, is to improve the quality of services, programming and internal processes at our institution, and its **value** is truly exceptional. "A truly exceptional college recognizes that every part of the organization contributes a key component to student success," says SUNY JCC's Vice President for Academic Affairs, Dr. Marilyn Zagora. "Thus, organizational excellence depends upon a commitment to quality and continuous improvement made and refreshed regularly by each unit."

Our FAR process was actually modeled after our academic program review process, which has been around for decades. Our guidelines state, the **"functional area review is a process of evaluating to**

what extent a service or program has been successful in achieving its intended goals, through systematic collection and analysis of information relevant to those goals." This practice is admittedly still in its infancy, as we are just concluding our third cohort of participants. I was among the first cohort in 2011-12, and while I was not new to the student affairs field, it was an intimidating undertaking at first. It ended up being an unprecedented opportunity for me to begin my tenure as director of campus life with a comprehensive audit of my department's history, functions, and strategic directions.

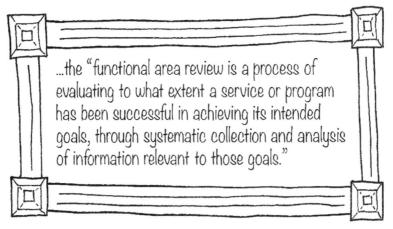

...the "functional area review is a process of evaluating to what extent a service or program has been successful in achieving its intended goals, through systematic collection and analysis of information relevant to those goals."

"The FAR process, while rigorous and sometimes challenging, is really designed to allow each unit time to reflect, refocus, and position itself to achieve at even higher levels of accomplishment," says Zagora. "In spotlighting each unit through a FAR, we give that group the chance to focus organizational attention to their needs, and, more importantly, to allow the college to see more clearly the assets of that area and the opportunities that area can offer to the college to further support student learning and success."

The functional area review process should produce (as appropriate):

- Objective data on which to base programmatic or area decisions
- Formal recommendations for the functional areas that are reached by the joint participation and input from faculty, staff, administration, and external review teams
- Action plans for accomplishing the above recommendations
- Directions for renewal and development
- Priorities for resource use
- A programmatic self-study
- A review of processes and procedures
- Input into sub plans
- An on-going process that uses data for continuous improvement

Functional areas that complete the process in the time allotted (one year) are eligible for up to $1,200 to support a recommendation identified through the FAR process. When I went through the FAR process, one of our recommendations necessitated we collect better data on who attends our events so we could in turn better assess the intended outcomes of our programs. We purchased handheld ID scanners with our funds that now enable us to swipe student ID cards and thereby track if our attendees are freshmen or sophomores, who lives on or off campus, how old they are, what their major is, and how many credits they've completed. We then assess this data for patterns to confirm and improve our quality of programming.

But let me back up. **WHY does SUNY JCC even have the Functional Area Review process?**

In 2008, Jamestown Community College formed an **Institutional Effectiveness Committee** in preparation for its Middle States re-accreditation visit expected spring 2011. Each of the 14 Middle States standards for accreditation was assigned to a sub-committee for internal review. In recent years, lots of institutions of higher education have received poor marks on

Standard 2: Planning, Resource Allocation, and Institutional Renewal; **Standard 7**: Institutional Assessment; and **Standard 14**: Assessment of Student Learning. In anticipation of these areas receiving close examination, the Institutional Effectiveness Committee observed that our college was "missing **a mechanism to systematically organize goals,**" says Barbara Russell, Dean of Institutional Research at SUNY JCC. Thus, to meet Standard 7 head on, JCC's Functional Area Review process was piloted.

The Functional Area Review at SUNY JCC has **three major phases** and each functional area is scheduled to undergo a FAR every five years:

1.) Internal Review Team
2.) External Review Team
3.) Closing the Loop

During the **Internal Review** phase, the department undergoing review assembles a core group of individuals from within the department and at least one colleague from outside the department at the institution. The internal team conducts self-assessments of its programs, services, and processes and determines self-directed priorities for the next five years. The internal team also produces a preliminary report that is archived at the institution and shared with the external review team to help them prepare for their visit.

The **External Review Team** visits are by far the most energetic part of the process, say both Zagora and Russell. The internal team selects three or four external reviewers from comparable institutions and invites these individuals to come to our institution to conduct focus groups and interviews that ultimately provide the internal team with recommendations. Fantastic conversations stem from these visits that bring energy and excitement to the overall assessment process. **The momentum of the FAR process is in fact sustained by the human interaction and educated dialogues sparked by these fresh set of eyes, says Zagora.** External review team members usually visit for one or two days and receive mileage, meals, and accommodations – an indication of true investment by the institution to this process.

The third and last phase, **Closing the Loop**, involves the FAR leader (usually the department director) compiling all the recommendations from both the internal and external teams and reviewing these with their supervisor for **feasibility, viability, and appropriateness.** The recommendations that are pursued are slotted for completion over the next five years. These recommendations are certainly not the only goals pursued for the foreseeable future, but they chart an initial course.

As with every young initiative, we've learned some lessons along the way. Here are a few reflections from our vice president of academic affairs. First, Zagora says, there needs to be **time and space to support the FAR team leaders individually and as a cohort.** From the start, our dean of institutional research gathered each unit's FAR leader in a meeting about once a month to discuss progress and answer questions that were arising during the year-long process. The academic program review side has since copied this practice. Second, Zagora believes better **public celebration of the work accomplished** by the units who've complete the process is needed so everyone at the institution on both sides of the house are more aware of the outcomes. Third, Zagora says **it's not enough to simply set goals as a functional area;** there needs to be a standard across all units for regular and systematic assessment. For us, this is the Functional Area Review.

My experience with this process was positive and valuable. Since conducting my own FAR, I've been asked to serve on the internal review team for other departments every year. Next year, our Campus Life department will be undergoing its second Functional Area Review. It is my hope that readers use this outline to spark conversations about accountability to the planning process at your home institutions just as we do.

Kim Irland is the Director of Campus Life at Jamestown Community College. She earned her graduate degree in Student Affairs & Diversity from Binghamton University where she worked as the graduate assistant for the XCEL Center for Student Leadership and as a graduate intern for New Student Orientation. Kim and her husband live in J amestown, NY with their two kids and two dogs. Follow her on Twitter @Kimantics.

DATA as STORYTELLING

Data as Storytelling - Lesley D'Souza

Storytelling is by no means a new concept. Humans have been using stories to educate, entertain, and remember for thousands of years because stories stick with us. They attach themselves to the emotional centre of our brain (our limbic brain if you're a Sinek fan) and help us to contextualize and process things that are happening in our lives now. The saying "those who forget history are doomed to repeat it" is frighteningly and demonstrably true. So how does this relate to assessment?

We know data is important to decision making. It's how we record and learn from our experiences so we aren't doomed to repeat our failures. The problem is that not everyone connects with numbers or Spartan facts. **We can gather and report our data until we're exhausted, but it won't make a difference if people aren't hearing us. We need to translate it into a story to help others**

feel the impact of our results. This involves telling people what our data means, and to do that we'll have to make meaning of it ourselves. If you are "not a numbers person", then you're also an ideal candidate to weigh in on what kind of story will appeal to the widest audience. So start by asking yourself what kind of story you would be interested in hearing.

It can be difficult to look at raw data and manage feelings of apprehension. If you're facing a screen of stats and numbers (a.k.a. quantitative data), you might not know where to begin when constructing a story, but if you dig deep there is one there, waiting to be told.

> What were your original goals? Did you meet them? Why or why not?
>
> If the participants represented certain demographics, why might that be? Who was missing, and why?
>
> What does the data tell you about the experiences that participants had? What did they walk away with?

All of these questions, when applied to your data, can help you form a story. **The key to making it a compelling story is to make it human and relatable.**

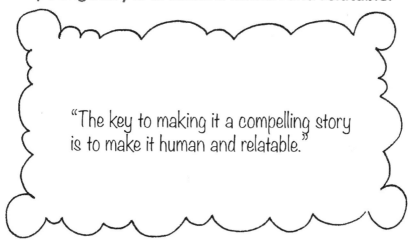

"The key to making it a compelling story is to make it human and relatable."

Technology today also gives us access to technology that is designed to help us tell our stories. Once you've found your compelling and relatable tale, put good use to media like images, infographics, videos, or social media, in addition to formal reports, to help get your information out there. **The sharing of your data is just as important as the gathering itself;** after spending all that time and effort collecting it, what was the point if you never get around to reporting and sharing it? From a different point of view, if you never share the stories that are hiding in your data, you'll never convince decision-makers that you are a) uniquely good at what you do, and b) worthy of additional resources to do more. This is your chance to shine light on your work and potentially offer a dissenting perspective that is vital to growth.

But that's not the only story here (pun intended). There are two sides to how storytelling fits into assessment: **our ability to tell stories as a result of data we've gathered,** but also, **our ability to gather stories that will provide data.** Yes, stories and narratives can be data themselves; if you're gathering them, you're conducting **qualitative assessment.** You might be collecting stories from interviews, written reflections, focus groups, or through observation. This kind of assessment gets a bad rap for not being as generalizable as quantitative data, but it gives us a valuable window into the "how" and "why" that quantitative assessment can't. It also evokes that human element that makes data so compelling and relatable. It's much easier to tell stories about your data when it's already in story-form. That is why it is important to have variety in our assessment methods— so our data speaks to everyone.

I think my favorite part of gathering stories is that **the simple act of asking a student to tell their story can be a transformative experience for them—and for us.**

Think about it: telling a story about yourself requires a great deal of self-reflection and vulnerability. And by asking for a student's perspective, we inherently validate them. This process can play a vital role in supporting students as they move through stages of identity development.

The final thought I want to leave you with is that **stories are incredibly powerful.** We can change opinions and beliefs with them, and we have access to storytelling tools barely dreamt of by past generations. It's funny—I used to think assessment had two purposes: to provide accountability, and to facilitate improvement. But I've found a third. **We can address social injustice by practicing mindfulness in the stories we choose to tell.** We can ask for stories from those who feel silenced and not only empower them, but give them access to a larger audience. By working in student affairs, we are in a position of remarkable privilege, and how we choose to use our influence will define our success. Our campuses are breeding grounds for the ideas of tomorrow. **If we commit to using our power to tell the right stories, maybe we can change our campuses— and then the world.**

 Lesley is the Student Life Programs Coordinator at Ryerson. She is a passionate, data-driven Student Affairs Professional with an MA in College Student Personnel who loves stories and empowering self-authorship in students. She's the mother of two wonderful boys and an avid gardener, tea drinker, musician and random fact junkie. Ask her anything! She hopes to write a book someday, do her PhD and inspire others. Tweeting from @lesleydsz.

LET'S THINK LIKE TEACHERS

Let's Think Like Teachers - Vicki L. Wise

Are student affairs practitioners viewing their work in the context of a student-learning framework? We know that the Council for the Advancement of Standards (CAS) has identified 44 functional areas in their standards for higher education programs and services (CAS, 2015). Student-learning occurs across all of these 44 areas, even in places we may think are least likely such as financial aid, registration and records, student legal services, and auxiliary services, to name a few. **All student affairs departments need to view their work through the lens of teaching and learning and use assessment to demonstrate their impact on student learning, and to improve programs and services.**

I come to this idea, in part, because I believe that student affairs practitioners are not always viewed by themselves, or others, as **educators**. So, what if we used some tools from K-12 educators' playbook? Both Grant Wiggins and Jay McTighe have written extensively about backward design in K-12 education. In Understanding by Design: A Framework for Effecting Curricular Development and Assessment, Wiggins and McTighe (2006) present a framework that integrates content and meaningful assessment with effective pedagogy to affect change in student knowledge, skills, and abilities. Essentially this means that **we start with the end in mind — the intended results of our efforts — and build the teaching and learning environment around these efforts.** This framework has long been used in K-12 education and is part of all teacher education programs. It needs to be part of all student affairs work too.

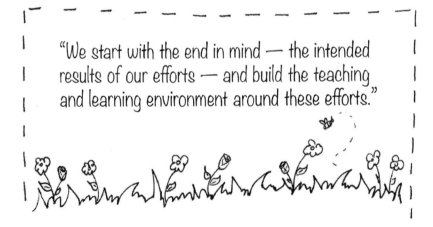

"We start with the end in mind — the intended results of our efforts — and build the teaching and learning environment around these efforts."

So how would their framework look in practice in our student affairs programs and services? In the first stage, **educators would identify the desired student** outcomes before outlining specifics of the program content and delivery. What should students know, understand, and be able to do as a result of engaging in programs and services? Be intentional but realistic as to the impact of your programs and services. If you want a change in student learning or a change in student behavior, a program of short duration will probably not make that kind of impact.

In the next stage, **determine what constitutes acceptable and meaningful evidence that students have achieved the desired outcomes. Decide how you will directly measure student learning.** Use a variety of the assessment tools available and consider using a combination of assessment approaches to measure student learning. This includes gathering evidence through research papers and other process reports, multiple choice or essay examinations, personal essays, journals, computational exercises and problems, case studies, audiotapes, videotapes, and short-answer quizzes, to name a few.

Finally in the last stage, **you will plan and deliver learning experiences and activities (curriculum) that will equip students with the desired knowledge and skills to meet the expected outcomes.** This alignment between expected outcomes, assessment, content and delivery constitute best practice. When these are aligned, educators use assessment to improve the learning experience for students who participate in programs and services.

What would student affairs practice look like under this model? Such practice **could integrate student affairs more into academic and university culture** by removing some of the silos that exist both within student affairs and across the campus. It will **foster professional development of student affairs practitioners in key areas** (Assessment, Evaluation, and Research and Student Learning and Development) endorsed in the ACPA and NASPA Professional Competency Areas for Student Affairs Practitioners (2010). Most importantly, **it would allow student affairs programs and services to tell their stories with even more credibility** so that when stakeholders are questioning the worth and value of a degree, given the financial costs to students and their families, they won't think of student affairs an auxiliary set of services.

 Vicki L. Wise, Ph.D. is the Associate Director for Teaching, Learning and Assessment at Portland State University. She has also served as Director for Assessment & Research at Portland State University in Student Affairs. Her areas of research include: scale development and improved measurement processes, assessment efficacy, scholarship in higher education, employee evaluation, and sustainability assessment. You can contact her at wisevl@pdx.edu.

I Strongly Agree that the Likert Scale Doesn't Work -

Matthew Cummings

One of the most important things you can do as an innovative professional in any career is to identify the emerging trends in your field and learn the skills associated with these trends. Your goal should be to make yourself indispensable and the best at what you do. I did not come from a Student Affairs or Higher Education background; during both my graduate and undergraduate experience, I majored in Urban Studies. I was interested in topics like: how do we motivate people for community development and how do we work around issues like poverty, racism, and classism for social change. I also learned about finances and program evaluation in the nonprofit sector. My work in Higher Education started when I was placed in a Civic Engagement Center as an AmeriCorps member and I started seeing the value of student volunteerism and long-term community development. I currently work at DePauw University as the Assistant Director of Spiritual Life, Community Service, and Social Justice, in which I interact with these three departments doing assessment work. **As soon as I started my career in Higher Education, the assessment demand clicked with me because I had previously studied program evaluation in the nonprofit sector and was versed in creating evidence surrounding goals and expected outcomes, since this was something constantly in demand for grants and fundraising.**

So as I began my work in Higher Education, I saw the demand for assessment skills and started to seek out books and conferences that would further equip me with this knowledge. I took the initiative of bringing this to our office and getting our team on track with assessment projects. **I'll be 100% honest and admit that we have had some challenges but also some success as we started office wide assessment.** The challenges have been in the process of creating buy-in and getting staff members to recognize the importance of continually building a culture of evidence around their programs through blogs, number tracking, and documenting conversations. The successes have been that we were able to start telling our story better and that folks who have worked in those departments even discussed how the process really challenged them to think about student learning.

So with all that said, there is still a lot of needed movement in the work of assessment and our institutions. I wanted to share some thoughts that I have observed from Facebook groups, Twitter, Conferences and other things.

The Likert Scale Sucks.

I have to admit that I have a love/hate relationship with the Likert Scale. I almost jumped with joy when our institutional research director sent me our old National Survey of Student Engagement (NSSE) data so I could attempt to measure the impact of service learning and deep learning from a conference presentation I heard at the IUPUI Assessment Conference. On top of my love for regression analytics, pivot tables, and Venn Diagrams, **a deep enthrallment enters my brain when I get an Excel sheet full of 1s, 2s, 3s, 4s, and 5s,** all representing different Likert responses. However, as the data comes to life, **I have to wonder if we are really**

demonstrating student learning through these questions.

Throughout my undergraduate and graduate experience, **never once in class have faculty asked if I "Strongly Agree, Agree, Disagree, or Strongly Disagree"** that I understood the basics of servant-leadership philosophy. Instead, our faculty friends would ask something in the nature of "Describe the core principles of servant-leadership philosophy." The open-ended wording of this question allows the participant to unpack all the knowledge that they can about the subject, while the Likert-based version only allows the student to unpack what they *think* they *might* know. **The purpose of an assessment question is not to measure satisfaction** (95% of students reported having a positive experience) **but to demonstrate the learning that takes place during the event** (I learned xyz through this...).

So what do we have to do? **Ask open-ended questions** that are connected to your student learning outcomes. If the information is not relevant to your program or your center's learning outcome, do not ask it! While it's much easier to score 1s and 3s on an Excel sheet than identifying themes in essays, you will have access to better data and will be doing more authenticity-driven assessment.

Your Pre-Test/Post-Test is pointless.

Let's also drop the pre-test and post-test. **Growth in knowledge should be expected after completing any structured activity where content is given**.

I mean, think about this for a second. Let's say you have never seen the movie Titanic. You're in a learning environment and the instructor asks you to write everything you know about the Titanic. You really don't know a lot about the story except for that part of the boat sinking. After a few hours of watching the movie with your peers and potentially shedding a few tears, your instructor now asks a question like "What did you learn about the Titanic after watching the movie?" Of course you will now have knowledge in this topic and be able to discuss in more detail the socio-economic class and the power structures of the boat. Of course your knowledge based has increased; this is what is to be expected and is far from a source demonstrating knowledge gained. I have literally seen people ask questions using a scale that said something like: Rate your basis of knowledge on the Titanic with a 1-5 (Low being a one, high being a Five) and then ask this question before and after the test. They then proceeded with great joy and success on how their event was a solid learning experience because the average jumped from 1.5 to 3.5 before and after. There was no qualitative portion or reflective component, just a couple scales utilizing means. **How many programs are substituting the word "Leadership" for "Titanic" and then calling their "assessment" student learning?**

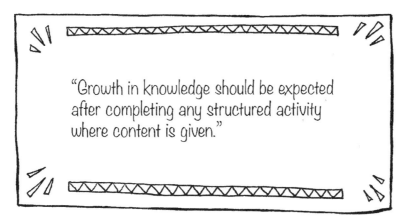

"Growth in knowledge should be expected after completing any structured activity where content is given."

On top of the tendency for people to self-report at higher rates of knowledge than they actually have, I'm just not convinced this is our best opportunity for data. Instead of the pre-test and post-test, perhaps we should implement writing prompts immediately after an event and another a month later to see how knowledge was gained and retained. Further, what if we use a retrospective method **that asks immediately what we learned but also at the same time asks us to reflect back and rate our knowledge prior to the event?**

Get Visual/Digital or GTFO.

Learn to communicate digitally. Ugly basic pie charts from Excel are cool and all and go a step further than what some people are doing, but there are many free and easy ways to communicate your data. Check out a website like Piktochart that incorporates beautiful charts and infographs through a simplified click and drag/drop method. As millennials we are a "tl;dr" culture. We want visual data minus the wall of text. **Figure out how to communicate your assessment results using a couple charts, some numbers, and a quote or two from students.** If you find yourself writing three for four sentences about your results on a one-sheet flyer, you're doing too much.

Make videos, use social media, post things to your Facebook page. Use your data as a vital part of your department's branding. Send your new beautiful reports to your VP and student leaders. Let development and communications know about your success. **Use your data as part of building your brand on your campus. Students want to be part of train that moves with success.**

Our office has received close to $150,000 in grants and donations from donors, foundations, and public agencies over the last year in which data and evidence played a vital role in us receiving these funds. At a recent Board of Trustees meeting, we were asked about numbers, hours, and benchmarks. People want to know both the numbers and stories associated with your office. **It's up to you recognize this trend and move forward.**

Matt holds a Masters of Arts in Urban Studies and Community Development from Eastern University and enjoys how student volunteerism, service-learning, and civic engagement plays an integral part in local and global community enhancement. At DePauw University, Matt is the Assistant Director of Spirituality, Service, and Social Justice in which he helps connect students to service opportunities, leads office wide program assessment and evaluation, and is always enthralled with tech news and apps.

Assessment is here to stay

Assessment is Here To Stay - Lesley D'Souza

When I attended ACPA in Tampa last year, I remember feeling a glow when I looked at the program because it was (almost) possible to attend a presentation on assessment during every concurrent session. Assessment has long been an interest and passion of mine, which sounds weird to say out loud. In fact, when I've talked about it to other Student Affairs professionals, sometimes the look they give me makes me think I've said something akin to "I love doing laundry." But it's true. **I love the puzzles presented by data and the search for it, and I revel in decoding patterns and trends from results.**

Canadians, like our US colleagues, drank the assessment kool-aid (it's delicious after all), but it seems like our current is cresting a little behind the assessment movement that I've seen in the US. We are committed, but still defining what that commitment looks like in our own culture of education. So, when I had the pleasure of reading **John Schuh's article,** "Assessment in Student Affairs: How Did We Get Here?" in the new Journal of Student Affairs Inquiry, it gave me a contextual window into the development of a Student Affairs-wide culture of assessment. **I found his analysis and thoughts, on where we've been and where we're going, spot on.**

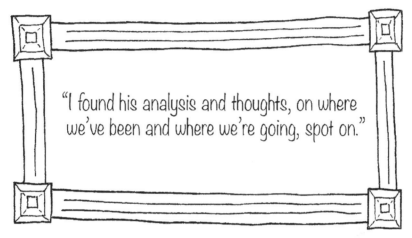

"I found his analysis and thoughts, on where we've been and where we're going, spot on."

The article begins with an extensive review of literature over the past 80 years, going back to the beginnings of Student Affairs as a field in the U.S. Though there are indirect and slight references to research and evaluation in the context of Student Affairs for the first decades, Schuh demonstrates a continually intensifying focus on assessment in publications relevant to our field, first recognizable in the 1990s. After "Learning Reconsidered" and Upcraft & Schuh's own "Assessment in Student Affairs" were published, **there is a veritable** landslide of literature that herald assessment as a central tenet to creating and maintaining good learning environments. He also references Project DEEP – and highlights those institutions with higher than expected graduation rates & NSSE scores that also demonstrated a commitment to data-informed decision-making.

Schuh finishes his article with a succinct trio of theses about the current status of assessment. He posits that:

1) Assessment is a newcomer to the scene,
2) That it serves two purposes at present: accountability & improvement, and
3) That it is a permanent fixture within Student Affairs.

He writes passionately that those who do not integrate assessment practices into their work do so at their peril, as "the future will be replete with assessment projects."

This piece is a valuable addition to the landscape of assessment in Student Affairs. By recognizing that a culture of assessment at our own institutions is key to finding success in using data for accountability & improvement, we must also understand the context in

which our own field's culture of assessment began. The final proposition by Schuh, that assessment is here to stay, is self-evident by the time you read it. You can see that it is true by looking back over our history. How often have we decried the gulf between Student and Academic Affairs? We can see that gap closing as we provide valid data showing the value of the learning we curate. It turns out that one of the most significant difference between us has been a lack of systematic assessment on our part.

I fully agree with his three final thoughts. Assessment is a term that's been tossed around since I was in grad school over ten years ago, but it seems to have snowballed since then. I hear everyone talking about it, or (unfortunately) worrying about, it these days. While I wouldn't call it a new idea, the widespread adoption of it is new.

Though not specifically stated as separate in his article, I believe the two purposes of assessment that Schuh outlined should not be conducted independently. In my opinion, they are inextricably linked as two products within a successful cycle of assessment. **We should assess learning by asking if we achieved that which we set out to do.** Once we have that information, **how**

could we avoid using it to make ourselves better during the following cycle? If we conduct assessment with only one of these purposes in mind, we're wasting a valuable opportunity to make the most of our data.

Finally, Schuh is absolutely correct. **Assessment is here to stay** – though I can understand how the rapid expansion of our culture of assessment has induced anxiety in those new to its practices. There is also the subsequent hope that it's a fad, soon to die out. **By looking at the history he has painstakingly assembled, it's obvious that this was a practice missing from the fabric of our work – to our detriment.**

We're finally coming to a place of validation and recognition from outside our field, and I can foresee a future in Student Affairs where assessment is a fundamental part of all job descriptions, preparatory programs, and practice. **And if you're trying not to think about assessment, consider yourself warned, because like Schuh says, "if not today, then certainly tomorrow."**

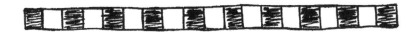

 *Lesley is the Student Life Programs Coordinator at Ryerson. She is a passionate, data-driven Student Affairs Professional with an MA in College Student Personnel who loves stories and empowering self-authorship in students. She's the mother of two wonderful boys and an avid gardener, tea drinker, musician and random fact junkie. Ask her anything! She hopes to write a book someday, do her PhD and inspire others. Tweeting from @lesleydsz.*

ASSESSING *First Year Experience*
COURSE ASSISTANTS, AN EXAMPLE

Assessing First Year Experience Course Assistants, an Example - Hallie Crawford

Like it or not, assessment is part of nearly every aspect of student affairs. When I was in graduate school and learning all about assessment, my supervisor was the departmental Coordinator for Assessment. Cha-ching! She helped take something very abstract and made it manageable. **Using simple steps and a current example, hopefully this article will do the same for you.**

"Using simple steps and a current example, hopefully this article will do the same for you."

I oversee programmatic aspects of our First Year Experience (FYE), including a required class for new students. Each class has an instructor and undergraduate course assistant (CA). Currently, each faculty/CA pair decides on CA responsibilities for their section. Some establish clear responsibilities. Others struggle with this, resulting in varying experiences between CAs. My goal is to clearly define the CA role and focus on student development, but before this can happen, I must collect feedback from current CAs through a nine-question survey.

Following an eight-step process, here's what my project looks like:

1. **GOALS**. Always set goals before you begin. Mine are:
   - Learn why students want to be a CA
   - Learn about current CA responsibilities
   - Develop CA training

2. **NEED**. This project is important because:

We recently welcomed our largest-ever freshman class. However, more students do not mean more faculty/staff. Now more than ever, student-leaders are vital to the success of our programs and services. Defining exactly what a CA does will maximize their capacity to assist FYE.

Our students value leadership opportunities. The CA role could be an excellent one. Currently, we are doing the CAs a disservice by not providing structure and learning.

Focusing on CAs is valuable because they have a unique relationship with first-year students. They are often close in age, recently sat in the same seat, and work closely with faculty and staff. Thus, CAs can provide faculty/staff with trends, ideas, concerns, and questions about FYE. Informal assessment – another cha-ching!

3. **TIMELINE**. This will vary depending on the project. My survey method is simple. I started the project in mid-October. Each CA received a survey, due November 13. Changes will begin in late spring, carrying through next academic year.

4. **ACTION STRATEGIES**. Based on conversations and early survey responses, trends are emerging. Trends inform action.

Many faculty members admittedly struggled using their CA. I will create a session for FYE faculty training about expectations and suggestions for utilizing a CA.

CAs want training and leadership development. A one-day training will include sessions on leadership, important policies, and professional communication. Survey responses will shape training sessions throughout the year.

5. **IDENTIFY KEY STAKEHOLDERS.** I started at Lenoir-Rhyne in August 2015. Being new, I needed to build relationships. When my supervisor told me the CA position needed attention, I scheduled meetings with faculty and staff close to FYE. By hearing their input and sharing ideas, I gained information and support.

6. **IMPLEMENTATION.** In an ideal world, every response to every assessment ever would become action. But we live in a world with budgets and unrealistic requests. It is important to discern what needs to, can, and just ain't gonna happen. To make these decisions, look for

trends and ask the right questions. Then determine short- and long-term plans. As mentioned, I will focus on a clear position description and training, and then go from there.

7. **FOLLOW-UP ITEMS.** Said training topics are a great example of follow-up items. For example, if CAs ask for certain trainings, I will provide it. Then, I'll ask for feedback on that training. Additionally, I will provide updates to stakeholders along the way – thank participants; share plans; be transparent. People appreciate when their voices are heard.

8. **REPORT**! Assessment reports can secure funding, recruit new students, and create opportunities for learning, among other things. When your data becomes a report, share it. If data proves your program valuable, you may have an easier time keeping and growing resources. If your program isn't effective, don't be afraid to change or cut it. The report on CA feedback will directly influence the short- and long-term development of the position, which has a huge potential impact on FYE.

If you're new to assessment, don't be scared. Start small. Focus on what you want to find. There are many assessment methods – choose one that matches your goals but is comfortable. **And most importantly, use what you find!**

Hallie K. Crawford, M.Ed is a proud alum of the Student Personnel Administration for Higher Education (SPAHE) program at UNC-Greensboro ('14) and The Ohio State University (BA, '12). She is wife to a college basketball coach and mom to #BogoTheDog. Hallie enjoys leadership education, working with student-athletes, and helping students reach their potential. Off campus, she loves to cook, read, and explore whatever state she's currently residing in with her husband and dog. Follow her @hk_crawf on Twitter.

"CAN I QUOTE YOU ON THAT?"

adding credibility

Can I Quote You on That? – Adding Credibility - Jeff

Burrow

Finally! Your assessment project is almost done. You had a goal, designed a project, collected and analyzed your data from (let's say) five focus student groups. And now you have written up a report including some implications and suggestions for change, and are ready to share with your team and to start talking about next steps.

But wait! **The analyzing and writing process can take several weeks or months, meaning that there is a large gap between when you 'heard' the student voices in the focus groups and when you finish a summary and interpretation of what they shared.** And in this process of preparing a draft report, what might have seemed very important initially can become a bit less clear and evident as you are immersed in all the data. Remember

96

that, in trying to summarize data from focus groups and interview, we must try to ensure that what we report on is based upon an accurate representation of what the students shared with us. There are lots of ways to help ensure a fair representation of the data from the students, like having **audio transcripts** and **taking personal notes**, but there are two other steps (that don't take very long) and can add to the trustworthiness and credibility of your final reports.

Member Check

One approach is to **share a summary of the key findings, themes and representative quotes with your participants.** This is often called a member check. In this case we are asking the members (students in the focus groups) if they "see" themselves in the findings and summaries you have created. You want them to tell you what you got right and what you might have (unintentionally) under or overstated. This process also gives the students one more chance to share with you. Why is this extra reflection useful? Think about how many times you have been in an interview or conversation and then later had that feeling afterwards of "Why didn't I mention that?" Using this process, you get the benefit of their feedback for accuracy and the time they have had to reflect on the focus group discussion.

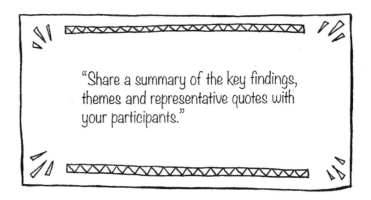

"Share a summary of the key findings, themes and representative quotes with your participants."

Peer Debriefing

A second approach is to **share your transcripts with a colleague who is acting as a "peer debriefer."** Ask them to read the transcripts, or whatever summaries of the focus groups you have. Have your colleague identify what they think the major findings are from these same conversations. This can be helpful to check against some of our own bias and potential blind spots. Who should you choose to help out? A good person to ask is someone who knows of but isn't totally involved in your program. When they have shared back with you, you can then discuss where your interpretations are aligned and where they might diverge. This process will not likely lead to total agreement, and it may lead to some re-writing on your part. However, it is a very useful step that should make you even more confident that what you share with your team, the data you use to inform decisions about what to do and not do, are based on the best analysis possible.

These are two ways we can help to ensure that the process we use to learn more about our programs and services results in the fairest representation of the stories the students share before we begin to make changes.

 Jeff Burrow is Manager, Analysis and Assessment and Co-chair of the Learning Outcomes and Assessment Committee in the Division of Student Life at the University of Toronto.He sees his role as both helping staff improve their assessment competence and confidence, understanding that virtually all student affairs staff have a natural desire to learn more about their programming impacts and the students they work with. Connect with him @jeff_burrow.

EVEN IF *you* FALL *on* YOUR FACE,

YOU ARE STILL MOVING FORWARD.

⟶

Even If You Fall On Your Face, You Are Still Moving
Forward - Renee Delgado Riley

Anyone who is responsible for assessment in student affairs understands the challenges of measuring the efficacy of our practices that are often unquantifiable. There are many research studies tackling assessment in higher education and specifically student affairs; however, assessment within student affairs often feels like running a marathon with little or no training. Many student affairs professionals are consistently trying to keep up with programs, student engagement, empowerment, being a life coach, that 'go to person' when our students are in distress and much more. How do we ever think about **assessment**? How many of us feel like we fall flat on our faces in this **assessment**

marathon even as we attempt to move **assessment forward**?

Well, Victor Kiam has the right idea — "Even if you fall on your face, you are still moving forward." That is right. It is better to keep on going even when we fall flat on our faces. Marathons have a finish line, but **assessment marathons** continue to cycle once we complete an assessment project. This drives the way we think about the activity, program or students we are assessing. Then the **assessment marathon** continues as we improve our practices.

Are you exhausted yet? We may not be provided with the ample assessment training or energy to integrate assessment within student affairs and often feel like throwing in the towel before we see the finish line, but it is critical that we build a **community of assessment practitioners** to help our colleagues move forward. This means helping each other get to the finish line and then making it an **assessment marathon relay** where our team members can help. There are many resources that we can use and share to help our colleagues along the way. For example, Student Affairs Assessment Leaders provides many templates, professional development and a **community of assessment practitioners** to learn from and is one of many available resources for Student Affairs professionals.

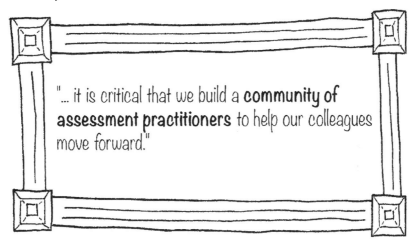

"... it is critical that we build a **community of assessment practitioners** to help our colleagues move forward."

NASPA's Assessment, Evaluation and Research Knowledge Community provides another forum to engage in this assessment marathon relay with others. There are many resources available nationally and locally, **but we have to be willing to work hard to support assessment within student affairs as a community of assessment practitioners because we cannot do this alone.** In order to move anything forward, we have to be willing to invest the time in our own professional development, but also to not forget that we are a community of student affairs professionals dedicated to student success.

Let's all help each other with assessment in student affairs by connecting each other to resources to have our best performance on our **assessment marathons**. As my new colleagues at the 2015 inaugural NASPA Escaleras Institute stated so clearly, "Sometimes you climb the ladder and sometimes you hold the ladder" (#Escaleras15). Happy assessing...and don't be scared to 'fall on your face' as that will be the only way you will move **assessment forward**.

Dr. Renee serves as the Director of Student Affairs Assessment & Research (SAAR) at the University of New Mexico. Her dissertation focused on understanding mathematics achievement gaps in elementary school between Hispanic and White students through multilevel growth models. She has worked at the University of New Mexico since 2009 and has an expertise in student services, assessment and staff development.

ENGAGING IN INQUIRY

The Big Picture: Engaging in Inquiry - Brian Bourke

Assessment. This word has become as ubiquitous in student affairs as bulletin boards and icebreakers. Each of us, regardless of position or functional area is increasingly asked (nudged) to engage in assessment work. There are lots of great resources to help understand what assessment entails, what it doesn't, and the areas we still need to address; I have provided a list of resources at the end of this chapter. What I hope to convey is a different perspective on why assessment work matters, and where we all need to expend more effort. **The area student affairs needs to address is connecting our assessment efforts to the institutional big picture.**

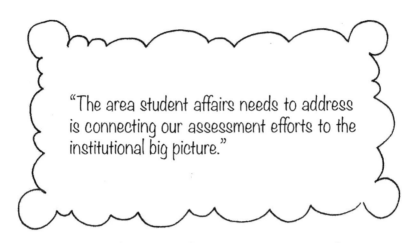

"The area student affairs needs to address is connecting our assessment efforts to the institutional big picture."

Big picture can be a bit of a nebulous term. There are a few ways to conceptualize institutional big picture in a way that makes sense for student affairs assessment work. We can attempt to force all of our pegs into the round holes of learning outcomes assessment, and in some case, learning outcomes are absolutely the correct method for assessing student experiences. The learning outcomes approach is gaining momentum as a way to connect assessment efforts across institutions. **When I teach assessment courses, something I stress to students is to make sure student affairs assessment is connected to the institution's mission and strategic plan.**

What matters most is understanding the institutional context and prevailing approaches to assessment that are most valued. We, as a field of scholar practitioners, need to address assessment holistically, rather than a collection of disconnected assessment measures. **One of the reasons this is important is the needed ability to respond to questions about the ways in which we serve students and affect learning.** We sometimes engage in moments of stomping our feet, beating our chests, and proclaiming our place in the academic enterprise. That place is one of equal importance to the academic side of the house, we proclaim. **If we are to ever support this claim, we have to prepare ourselves to defend it by demonstrating the role of student affairs-connected experiences to demonstrable measures of student learning.** This can only be accomplished by looking across the spectrum of data. This will tell us what we're doing well, and where we need to learn more.

Even beyond connecting specific assessment efforts to institutional big picture, **we need to think about assessment as an opportunity to learn and to engage in inquiry.** At a basic level, inquiry is about learning through seeking information. There is also a more nuanced perspective of inquiry that can be beneficial in helping us consider the implications of connecting our efforts to the institutional big picture. Inquiry can be defined as a conversation connecting community through questions. **If we draw on this definition of inquiry, and morph our disconnected assessment efforts into series of questions to which we seek answers collectively, we might be onto something.**

Calling our assessment efforts inquiry won't, by itself, make our inquiry connected to the institutional big picture. What matters is developing a culture in which assessment, evaluation, inquiry, whatever we call it, is not only valued, but also central to working in student affairs. Schein (2004) defined culture as "a pattern of shared basic assumptions that the group learned as it solved its problems of external adaptation and internal integration" (p. 17). If we approach developing a culture of inquiry or assessment using Schein's lens, we can situate ourselves, and our departments, to reflect the institutional big picture, **because our work of shaping the culture is embedded with learning.**

These resources reflect my go-to items for getting folks on the same page to have discussions about big-picture perspective on assessment:

- Assessment Essentials by Palomba & Banta (big why of assessment)
- The Invisible Tapestry by Kuh & Whitt (institutional culture)
- Assessment Reconsidered by Keeling, Wall, Dungy & Underhile

- Other sources of great information about assessment:
- NASPA Assessment, Evaluation and Research Knowledge Community
- ACPA Commission on Assessment & Evaluation
- Student Affairs Assessment Leaders

Brian has been faculty member of higher education and student affairs since 2007. In that time he has regularly taught courses focused on student affairs practice. You can regularly find him on Twitter advocating for assessment and professional development in student affairs, challenging you when you criticize #sagrad programs on the whole. Find him on twitter @drbbourke

An Interview with the Dean of Research and Planning - Kimberly Irland

I am very fortunate to have a phenomenal Office of Institutional Research at my disposal. Recently, I interviewed our Dean of Research and Planning, Barb Russell, about her thoughts on assessment in student affairs and what follows is a paraphrased transcript of our conversation.

1. Please define what assessment "dashboards" are and how these can be utilized by student affairs functional areas?

At Jamestown Community College, assessment dashboards are static periodic reports, which contain information on trends to help inform decision-making.

Currently, we offer dashboards to athletics, residence life, campus activities, orientation, and recruitment/admissions. We closely examine the relationship between different variables to measure retention rates, graduation rates, enrollment rates, and success rates at various critical junctures like six-week grades and census. **The goal is to use this data to improve processes and services provided by student affairs.** The bottom line for all assessment is to improve.

2. What groundwork do you recommend functional areas establish for efficient data collection?

As with all assessment, defining WHAT YOU WANT TO MEASURE is the first step. Ask yourself, what is the expected outcome of the activity? What do you NEED to know to improve the activity? **The key is to START with identifying how you will measure your learning outcome(s).** Examples of questions you can ask include, "what do you remember about...?" or "what did you learn from attending...?" And if you are doing any kind of training for student staff or student leaders, make sure you have a rubric in place beforehand to use for measuring whether or not the training was successful and effective.

3. What advice do you have for student affairs professionals working to develop student-learning outcomes for their programs and services?

Break programs and services into small pieces, i.e. "students attending this event should learn ___." **Then ask yourself HOW you can determine if they did in fact learn what you intended.** We are all very busy in higher education; so don't view assessment as a "new task." Incorporate this into what you already do. For example, if you already give students a satisfaction survey at the end of your program, add a question to that survey that asks them to articulate something they learned. Or add a multiple choice question if that is easier...Check all that apply, "what did you learn today?" or "what did you discover you did not know before XX event?"

4. What role do you see Offices of Institutional Research serving in the future for their student affairs colleagues at their institutions? How has this role changed from previous expectations?

We are a partner and a resource. Planning and goal writing have always been part of the charge for my student affairs colleagues, but in the current atmosphere of institutional effectiveness new light is being shone here. **All of higher education is expected to be engaging in a cycle of continuous improvement.** Emphasis is on data driven decision-making as limited resources are being further limited. Student learning outcomes outside the classroom are relatively new, but they are not going away. All the accreditation bodies are using similar language for their evaluation of these activities. So utilize your institution's office of institutional research staff and faculty who are experienced at assessing learning outcomes.

5. What assessment trends do you see developing that might be relevant for student affairs practitioners?

Use of BIG DATA is the current trend and I only see this growing. For example, researchers at the University of Rochester are using Instagram to track teen drinking. An example of "big data" collection on a college campus is when campuses track and review patterns from swiped IDs to make decisions. **With more technology being used by students, I see more and more assessment tracking being implemented.**

 Kim Irland is the Director of Campus Life at Jamestown Community College. She earned her graduate degree in Student Affairs & Diversity from Binghamton University where she worked as the graduate assistant for the XCEL Center for Student Leadership and as a graduate intern for New Student Orientation. Kim and her husband live in J amestown, NY with their two kids and two dogs. Follow her on Twitter @Kimantics.

114

Assessing the Your Neighbour Program, An Example -

Troy Murray & Brandon Smith

"Your Neighbour was a different learning experience. We got to learn about the importance of Ryerson's values and the fact that they're essential in any community. It's one thing to learn about values through theory, but going out, meeting different people and seeing the positive influence you can have on the community and what they can have on you is a great way to round off our August Training program and learn the true meaning of these values and what this means for community."

– Mohamed El Abshihy, Residence Advisor, ILLC

On August 27th, 2015, Ryerson Housing & Residence Life student leaders participated in a daylong learning experience called Your Neighbour, focused on Ryerson's values from the university's Academic Plan.

In order to do this, intentional curriculum was developed through the following learning outcomes, which were also used to provide framework and assess this learning experience. By participating in Your Neighbour, student leaders from Housing & Residence Life will be able to...

- (**ANALYSIS***) explore and critically examine how their intersecting identities (i.e.: student, community member of residence/Ryerson/Toronto, first-generation learner, gender/sex, etc.) are impacted by Ryerson's values through personal and group reflection activities.

- (**COMPREHENSION***) demonstrate and describe how Ryerson is building a culture of community engagement and philanthropy through group discussions with the partner organization.

- (**APPLICATION***) apply one value connected to the academic plan by integrating Ryerson's definition of this value to their experience from their off-campus visit through a culminating group presentation.

- (**SYNTHESIS***) manage an on-going community resource list, by area team, that includes existing community resources on-campus (i.e.: Tri-Mentoring program and Ambassador program) and organizations off-campus (not limited to those spaces visited) to refer to students interested or in-need of support, or through a support and action plan.

*NOTE: Learning Outcomes were guided by Bloom's Taxonomy.

Groups were divided early in the summer, allowing participants to express their own interest in learning more about each specific value. The groups were also intentionally divided to mix leadership positions and experience to invite cross-positional learning opportunities. This was advantageous to look at from an assessment standpoint, as each student-leader's position has a different connection to each of the values described in the academic plan; therefore, cross-positional learning opportunities allows for each person and position to provide new and different context for their own and their group's development. This also directly connected to our first learning outcome, focused on analysis.

The Your Neighbour experience continues to echo in our residence halls. We have referred to it beyond our training program, heard even more about it from our student leaders, and some student leaders have begun to develop their own experiences off campus to share with their communities. Our hope, and the next phase, is that Your Neighbour evolves into smaller community projects in and outside of residence that will further all of our students' out of classroom experience, and influence a culture of philanthropy with the understanding of our values—that we are members of the residence, Ryerson, and Toronto communities.

The next incarnation of Your Neighbour, however, will include all of our LLC students participating in an experience similar to the August 2015 program with the Residence Life Team, that begins their year with integrating into the new communities they are a part of in residence, at Ryerson, and in Toronto, before all of our students move into residence.

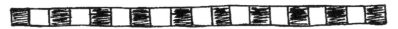

Troy is the Sponsorship & Fundraising Officer for Ryerson University's Student Affairs Department. He's responsible for seeking alternative sources of revenue and creating strategic partnerships to enhance student development. Follow him @TroyMurray22.

Brandon is Residence Life & Education Coordinator in Housing & Residence Life. He joined Ryerson in October. At Mac, he was also a Residence Manager (live-in position), and had this same role at Mount Royal University in Calgary, AB from 2008-2010.

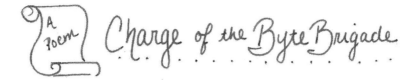

Charge of the Byte Brigade, A Poem - Dr. Gerry Crinnin

We sincerely hope you have enjoyed the reading this book. Thank you to all the contributors for your many incredible perspectives and valuable recommendations!

As a final thought to conclude our book, please enjoy a poem about assessment written by Dr. Gerry Crinnin of Jamestown Community College.

Charge of the Byte Brigade

Half a ream, half a ream,
Half a ream onward,
All in the Valley of Middle States
Wrote the one hundred.
"Assess, assess, do more with less!"
With a shared sense of urgency
into the Valley of Middle States
Wrote the one hundred.

"Advance to Middle States!"
Was there a plague of stomachaches?
Not that even the newest hiree felt
In any way encumbered;
Ours not to fall below,
Ours but to SLO,
Not to merely say but show:
Into the Valley of Middle States
Wrote the one hundred.

Files to the right of them,
Files to the left of them,
Files in front of them
Too many to be properly numbered
Stormed at with time crawling up their back:
Evidence the culture with a fact –
Trac Dis, Trac Dat!
Bolderly they entered data and collated,
Mission Critical into the jaws of Hell
Wrote the one hundred.

When can their glory fade?
Of the highest marks they made?
Oh, do not wonder.
We may consolidate, but sooner more than late

We will assemble a hundred other.

Professor of English at Jamestown Community College. Winner of SUNY Chancellor's Award for Creative and Scholarly Activity. He holds a PhD in English/Creative Writing.

Appendix

Assessment Tool for Regional and National Conferences

- Theresa Radley

The What!

The mission of The Association for the Promotion of Campus Activities (APCA) is to promote campus engagement through quality educational experiences, affordable entertainment and community service initiatives. APCA offers many opportunities for students and advisors to learn, serve, and network at regional and national conferences.

The Why!

For the past seven years, I attended the APCA Northeast Regional Conferences with a variety of students. I was fortunate to bring different students every time who are involved in a variety of student organizations. This allowed for as many students as possible to benefit from what APCA offers. However, no matter who came, or what student organization he/she was involved with, the results were always the same:

- Participating students knew the interest of their peers and thought critically about what programs will benefit the campus. They collaborated on programs with a variety of student organizations and departments including Multicultural Affairs, African-Latino Society and Active Minds.

- Participating students were more motivated to get involved in higher leadership positions and expand their comfort zones by joining new student organizations.
- Participating students met artists and agents that served as mentors to them.
- After years of witnessing so many success stories from the students who attended APCA, I knew I had to find a way to collect and present the data.

In Fall 2015, every department, under what was formally called "Student Affairs," was asked to create an assessment on a program we worked very closely with. I thought about the student organizations I advise, the leadership development workshops I host, and the students I mentor every day. I realized this was the opportunity I needed to showcase Ithaca College's APCA success stories on paper.

The How!

I spoke with Jondra Darden, who at the time was the Director of Engagement, about my idea. We discussed in detail about the learning outcomes. I knew from past experience learning that was occurring at APCA; however, I wanted staff to be included in the conversations as well. I developed four learning outcomes:

After attending the APCA Conference, students can:
- Identify different events/practices presented on other campuses
- Plan and produce creative and affordable events for their campus
- Demonstrate new leadership skills in leading their student organizations
- Create networking connections with participants from other schools and agencies

I worked very closely with an Ithaca College student, who attended APCA. She helped develop the tools of measurement and provided the student perspective. We wanted to develop different ways to measure the students learning to ensure all aspects of the conference experience were included. After every conference, we had already established a verbal wrap up on the last day of the conference. Therefore, I felt it would be best to add questions to the conversation more focused on assessment. The student and I developed a written survey for students to complete prior to leaving the conference. Each question applied to a learning outcome. I then developed a conference checklist to be completed by the advisor for each student after the trip, checking off all opportunities the students took advantage of at the conference. I developed a rubric to demonstrate the level that students were achieving the learning outcomes:

Ranking	Above Average	Average	Below Average
Identify different events/practices presented on other campuses	Student can identify different events/practices and ways our campus might incorporate them	Student listed different events/practices on campus but did not provide specific detail	Student cannot identify events at other campuses
Plan and produce an affordable event for the entire Ithaca College campus	Student planned events for student organization with the entire campus in mind and	Student focused primarily on their own student organization but did contribute to discussion	Student only planned events for their specific student organization

	brought back resources for other outlets on campus	about events for entire campus	
Demonstrate new leadership skills in leading their student organizations	Student can demonstrate new skills that they learned and how s/he will apply it to their student organization	Student can demonstrate leadership skills they learned but not clear how to apply it to their student organization	Student cannot demonstrate that they learned any new leadership skills
Create networking connections with participants from other schools and agents	Student can identify the connections they made and how they might be helpful in the future	Student can identify connections made at the conference but is unclear how they will be helpful in the future	Student cannot identify connections made at the conference

To demonstrate that APCA was providing students with knowledge and skills for the long-term, I developed another written survey for students to complete mid-way through the following semester after attending APCA.

After presenting the assessment to advisors at the APCA Advisor Institute, more learning outcomes were developed.

 Theresa is an educator before anything else. Education is her number one value and plans to continue educating not only students and her children, but herself as well. She currently serves as the Assistant Director of Student Involvement at Ithaca College where she has the privilege of teaching and learning from amazing students.

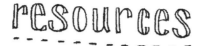

Resources

Overcoming the "I don't have time" Barrier

https://www.linkedin.com/pub/megan-forecki/10/610/94a

https://twitter.com/lucasschalewski

Four Stages of Assessment Competence

http://gavinhenning.com/2012/01/31/assessment-isnt-an-activity-its-a-state-of-mind/

https://attendee.gotowebinar.com/register/6741731780013024002

http://www.gordontraining.com/free-workplace-articles/learning-a-new-skill-is-easier-said-than-done/

http://www.myacpa.org/professional-competency-areas-student-affairs-practitioners

http://www.amazon.com/Leading-Assessment-Student-Success-

Practice/dp/1620362228/ref=mt_paperback?_encoding=UTF8&
me=

http://www.amazon.com/Coordinating-Student-Affairs-
Divisional-
Assessment/dp/1620363305/ref=sr_1_2?ie=UTF8&qid=144536
6525&sr=8-2&keywords=gavin+henning

www.myacpa.org/commae

https://www.naspa.org/constituent-groups/kcs/assessment-
evaluation-and-research

It Starts With Curiosity

http://ryersonstudentaffairs.com/

http://ryersonstudentaffairs.com/assessment-and-you/

http://ryersonstudentaffairs.com/ryersonsa-staff-
competencies/

http://ryersonstudentaffairs.com/ryersonsa-staff-
competencies/#assessment

Go FAR - The Functional Area Review

http://www.sunyjcc.edu/

intranet.sunyjcc.edu/sites/default/files/Functional_Area_Revie
w_Guidelines_20150420.pdf

http://www.msche.org/?Nav1=ABOUT&Nav2=MISSION

http://www.msche.org/publications/CHX-2011-WEB.pdf

Data as Storytelling

http://ryersonstudentaffairs.com/

http://ryersonstudentaffairs.com/assessment-and-you/

https://www.ted.com/talks/simon_sinek_how_great_leaders_i
nspire_action?language=en

Let's Think Like Teachers

http://www.lifescied.org/content/6/2/95.full.pdf

I Strongly Agree that the Likert Scale Doesn't Work

http://csl.iupui.edu/doc/teaching-research-assessment/research-brief-sept-2013.pdf

https://www.aacu.org/value-rubrics

http://www.uwex.edu/ces/pdande/resources/pdf/Tipsheet27.pdf

http://www.slideshare.net/mattwcummings/assessment-51981795

Assessment is Here To Stay

https://submissions.scholasticahq.com/login

https://submissions.scholasticahq.com/sites/the-journal-of-student-affairs-inquiry

http://www.naspa.org/publications/books/learning-reconsidered-a-campus-wide-focus-on-the-student-experience

http://as.wiley.com/WileyCDA/WileyTitle/productCd-0787902128.html

http://nsse.indiana.edu/html/projectDEEP.cfm

Charge of the Byte Brigade, A Poem

http://www.sunyjcc.edu/

http://www.sunyjcc.edu/faculty-staff-directory?field_first_name_value=&field_last_name_value=crinnin&field_academic_department_tid=All&field_job_type_value=All&field_primary_campus_tid=All

http://poetrybygerrycrinnin.weebly.com/

http://www.poetryfoundation.org/poem/174586

https://studentaffairscollective.org/saassess-assessment-bad-reputation-student-affairs/

https://studentaffairscollective.org/tag/saassess/

Even If You Fall On Your Face, You Are Still Moving Forward

http://studentaffairsassessment.org/

https://www.naspa.org/constituent-groups/kcs/assessment-evaluation-and-research

https://www.naspa.org/events/escaleras

Assessment and the Big Picture

http://www.naspa.org/constituent-groups/kcs/assessment-evaluation-and-research

http://www.myacpa.org/commae

http://studentaffairsassessment.org/

An Interview with the Dean of Research and Planning

http://www.sunyjcc.edu/faculty-staff-directory?field_first_name_value=&field_last_name_value=russell&field_academic_department_tid=All&field_job_type_value=All&field_primary_campus_tid=All

http://wxxinews.org/post/researchers-ur-use-instagram-track-teen-drinking-0

Assessing the Your Neighbour Program, An Example

http://ryersonstudentaffairs.com/your-neighbour-connecting-students-to-the-community/

https://juliaec.wordpress.com/2011/03/23/blooms-taxonomy-encouraging-higher-cognitive-thinking-in-primary-school-classrooms/

http://ryersonstudentaffairs.com/your-neighbour-assessment/

http://ryersonstudentaffairs.com/putting-ideas-into-action-housings-living-learning-program/

http://ryersonstudentaffairs.com/your-neighbour-assessment/

Here's To Your Continued Success!

a Student Affairs Collective book

63286862R00079

Made in the USA
Lexington, KY
02 May 2017